THE SANTALAND DIARIES and SEASON'S GREETINGS

BY DAVID SEDARIS

ADAPTED FOR THE STAGE
BY JOE MANTELLO

★

DRAMATISTS
PLAY SERVICE
INC.

THE SANTALAND DIARIES was produced by David Stone and Amy Nederlander-Case at the Atlantic Theater, in New York City, in November, 1996. It was directed by Joe Mantello; the set design was by Ian Falconer; the costume design was by Isaac Mizrahi; the lighting design was by Jan Kroeze; the sound design was by David Van Tieghem; and the production stage manager was Pamela Edington. It was performed by Timothy Olyphant.

TABLE OF CONTENTS

THE SANTALAND DIARIES

THE SANTALAND DIARIES

I was in a coffee shop looking through the want ads when I read, "Macy's Herald Square, the largest store in the world, has big opportunities for outgoing, fun-loving people of all shapes and sizes who want more than just a holiday job! Working as an elf in Macy's SantaLand means being at the center of the excitement...."

I circled the ad and then I laughed out loud. The man seated next to me turned on his stool, checking to see if I was a lunatic. I continued to laugh, quietly, until the check arrived and I remembered that I don't have a job. Funny how you can forget a thing like that.

I brought the ad home and my roommate Rusty and I were laughing about it and he dared me to call for an interview. So I did.

The woman at Macy's asked, "Would you be interested in full-time elf or evening and weekend elf?"

I said, "Full-time elf."

I have an appointment next Wednesday at noon.

I am a thirty-three-year-old man applying for a job as an elf.

I suppose it could be worse. I often see people on the streets dressed as objects and handing out leaflets. I tend to avoid leaflets but it breaks my heart to see a grown man dressed as a taco. So, if there is a costume involved, I tend not only to accept the leaflet, but to accept it graciously, saying, "Thank you so much," and thinking, "You poor, pathetic son of a bitch." This afternoon on Lexington Avenue, I accepted a leaflet from a man dressed as a camcorder. Hot dogs, peanuts, tacos, video cameras, these things make me sad because they don't have a place. They don't fit in on the streets. In a parade, maybe, but not on the streets. I figure that at least as an elf I will have a place; I'll be in Santa's Village with all the other elves. We will reside in a fluffy wonderland surrounded by candy canes and gingerbread shacks. It won't be quite as sad as standing on some street corner dressed as a French fry.

I am trying to look on the bright side. I arrived in New York three weeks ago with high hopes, hopes that have been challenged. In my imagination, I'd go straight from Penn Station to the offices of *One Life To Live*, where I would drop off my bags and spruce up before heading off for drinks with my new celebrity friends. Victoria Buchanan, the show's greatest star would lift her frosty glass in my direction and say, "Everyone, People, please, may I have your attention. I'd like to propose a toast to ... Clint, sit down, darling, this isn't about you. I'd like to propose a toast to our friend, David, the newest member of our television family. Welcome to Llanview!"

I'd say, "You guys, cut it out." Vicky would lay her hand over mine and tell me that I'd better get used to being the center of attention.

But instead I am applying for a job as an elf. Even worse than applying is the very real possibility that I will not be hired, that I couldn't even find work as an elf. That's when you know you're a failure.

I'm down to the wire here, twenty dollars away from walking dogs. After begging my mother for a loan I applied at a place that covers styrofoam creatures in moss. Left to its own devices, nature can cover things in moss. For free. It's not that difficult a task but still I didn't get the job. A skill. A person needs a skill. Why hadn't I ever realized that before?

10

In order to become an elf, I filled out ten pages' worth of forms, took a multiple choice personality test, underwent two interviews, and submitted urine for a drug test. The first interview was general, designed to eliminate the obvious sociopaths. During the second interview we were asked why we wanted to be elves, which, when you think about it, is a fairly tough question. I listened as the woman ahead of me, a former waitress, answered the question, saying, "I really want to be an elf? Because I think it's about acting? And before this I worked in a restaurant? Which was run by this really wonderful woman who had a dream to open a restaurant? And it made me realize that it's really really ... important to have a ... dream?"

Everything this woman said, every phrase and sentence, was punctuated with a question mark and the interviewer never raised an eyebrow.

When it was my turn I explained that I wanted to be an elf because it was one of the most frightening career opportunities I had ever come across. The interviewer raised her face from my application and said, "And...?"

I'm certain I failed my drug test. My urine had roaches and stems floating in it but still they called me back for another round of questioning. I met with the two head managers for a brief interview where they asked questions related to my interests and hobbies. I can't recall my exact words but somewhere along the line I expressed an interest in whittling. In truth the only thing I've ever whittled is a bong. I was just searching for something elf-like and figured I'd pulled it off when they sent me downstairs to fill out a series of tax forms. Afterwards I was sent to a holding pen where I took a seat beside a female dwarf. This, I thought, was a good sign. Names were called and the smallest people were summoned into the manager's office. After them went the guys with the biggest ears and the women without chins. I waited a long time. Just when I'd given up hope the manager cocked her finger and led me into her office where I was told, "Congratulations, Sir. You are an elf."

I have spent the last several days sitting in a crowded, windowless, Macy's classroom undergoing the first phases of Elf Training.

This morning we were lectured by the SantaLand managers and presented with a Xeroxed booklet of regulations titled, "The Elfin Guide." Most of the managers are former elves who have worked their way up the candy-cane ladder but retain vivid memories of their days in uniform. Several of the bosses led us in motivational cheers, a concept which stuns me to the core. One guy rolled up his sleeves and yelled, GIVE ME AN S! "S," WHERE'S MY A? "A!," HOW 'BOUT A BIG OL' N? "N," DID SOMEONE SAY T? "T," LET'S GET A RECALL ON THAT A! "A!" What's that spell? "SANTA!" WHO'S THE MAN?! "SANTA." COME ON ELVES, FEEL GOOD ABOUT YOURSELVES, LET'S RAISE THE ROOF!!! SANTA, SANTA SANTA! It was his goal to send chills down our spine and personally speaking, I think he did an excellent job. I was mortified.

They closed the meeting saying, "I want you to remember that even if you are assigned Photo Elf on a busy weekend, YOU ARE NOT SANTA'S SLAVE."

I spent the rest of my eight hour day with fifty elves and one perky, well meaning instructor in an enormous Macy's classroom, the walls of which were lined with NCR 2152's. A 2152, I have come to understand, is a cash register. The class was broken up into study groups and given assignments. My group included several returning elves and a few experienced cashiers who tried helping me by saying things like, "Don't you even know your personal ID code? Jesus, I had mine memorized by ten o'clock."

Everything about the cash register intimidates me. The worst part is that after I have accumulated three hundred dollars in my register, I have to remove two hundred, fill out half a dozen forms, and run the envelope of cash to the drop in the China Department or to the vault on the balcony above the first floor. I will not be allowed to change my clothes beforehand. I'll have to go dressed as an elf. An elf in Santa-Land is one thing, an elf in Sportswear is something else altogether.

Today we were told that during the second week of December, SantaLand is host to "Operation Special Children," at which time poor children receive free gifts donated by the store. There is another morning set aside for terribly sick and deformed children. On that day it is an elf's job to greet the child at the Magic Tree and jog back to the house to brace our Santa.

"The next one is missing a nose," or "Crystal has third-degree burns covering ninety percent of her body."

Missing a nose. With these children Santa has to be careful not to ask, "And what would *you* like for Christmas?"

Interpreters for the deaf came and taught us to sign "MERRY CHRISTMAS! I AM SANTA'S HELPER." They told us to speak as we sign and to use bold, clear voices and bright facial expressions. They taught us to say "YOU ARE A VERY PRETTY BOY/GIRL! I LOVE YOU! DO YOU WANT A SURPRISE?"

My sister Amy lives above a deaf girl and has learned quite a bit about sign language. She taught some to me and so now I am able to say, "SANTA HAS A TUMOR IN HIS HEAD THE

SIZE OF AN OLIVE. MAYBE IT WILL GO AWAY TOMOR-
ROW BUT I DON'T THINK SO."

This afternoon we were given a tour of SantaLand, which
really is something. It's beautiful, a real wonderland with ten
thousand sparkling lights, false snow, train sets, bridges, decorated trees, mechanical penguins and bears, and really tall
candy canes. We entered and traveled through an elaborate
maze, a path which takes you from one festive environment to
another. The charm faded when we were given code names for
some of the various stations. The narrow hallway beside the entrance is referred to as the "Oh My God" Corner. People arriving see the long line and say, "Oh my God," and it is an elf's
job to calm them down and explain that it will take no longer
than an hour to see Santa. Further along the path we came to
what is known as "The Vomit Corner," a mirrored wall where
nauseous children tend to surrender the contents of their
stomachs. When someone throws up, the nearest elf is instructed to yell, "VAMOOSE," the brand name of the janitorial
product used by the store. The path ends at The Magic Tree
which is supposed to resemble a complex system of roots. The
child is supposed to think, "I can't believe I'm inside a tree,"
but instead it looks like a large scale model of the human in-
testinal tract. Once you pass the tree, the lights dim and an elf
guides you to Santa's house which is actually more like a shack
in regards to size. There's no sink or toilet so it's hard to imag-
ine Santa actually living there. It's more like his den or his
think tank but they've gone out of their way to make the place
cozy and intimate, the walls lined with toys. Each house has a
hidden camera.

After the tour we were given a demonstration of the various positions in action, performed by returning elves who were
so animated and relentlessly cheerful that it embarrassed me

14

to walk past them. I don't know that I could look someone in the face and exclaim, "Oh, my goodness, I think I see Santa!" or "Can you close your eyes and make a very special Christmas wish!" Everything these elves said had an exclamation point at the end of it!!! It makes one's mouth hurt to speak with such forced merriment. I feel cornered when someone talks to me this way. Doesn't everyone? I prefer being frank with children. I'm more likely to say, "You look exhausted. Isn't this a school night?" or "I know a lot of people who would kill for that little waistline of yours."

I am afraid I won't be able to provide the grinding enthusiasm Santa is asking for. I think I'll be a low-key sort of an elf.

Today was elf dress rehearsal. The woman in charge of costuming assigned us our outfits and gave us a lecture on keeping things clean. She held up a calendar and said, "Ladies, you know what this is. Use it. I have scraped enough blood out from the crotches of elf knickers to last me the rest of my life. And don't tell me, 'I don't wear underpants, I'm a dancer.' You're not a dancer. If you were a real dancer you wouldn't be here. You're an elf and you're going to wear panties like an elf."

Elves have gotten to know one another over the past few days of training but once we took off our clothes and put on the uniforms, everything changed. This was really going to happen. *(He begins changing into costume.)*

My costume is green. I wear red and white striped tights, a yellow turtleneck, a forest-green velvet smock, and a perky stocking cap decorated with spangles. This is my work uniform.

During dress rehearsal, you have to go by your elf name. The other elves chose names like "Jingle" and "Frosty." They take the children by the hand and squeal with forced delight. They sing and prance and behave like cartoon characters come to life. It frightens me. My elf name is Crumpet.

Today was the official opening day of SantaLand. On any given day you can be an Entrance Elf, a Water Cooler Elf, a Bridge Elf, Train Elf, Maze Elf, Island Elf, Magic Window Elf, Emergency Exit Elf, Counter Elf, Magic Tree Elf, Pointer Elf, Santa Elf, Photo Elf, Usher Elf, Cash Register Elf, Runner Elf, or Exit Elf. I worked as a Magic Window Elf. I was at the Magic Window for fifteen minutes before a man approached me and said, "You look so fucking stupid." I have to admit that he had a point. But still, I wanted to say that at least I get paid to look stupid, that he gives it away for free. But I can't say things like that because I'm supposed to be merry.

So instead I said, "Thank You!"

"Thank you!" as if I had misunderstood and thought he had said, "You look terrific."

"Thank you!"

He was a brawny wise guy wearing a vinyl jacket and carrying a bag from Radio Shack. I should have said, real loud, "Sorry man, I don't date other guys."

The Magic Window, is really boring. I'm supposed to stand around and say, "Step on the Magic Star and look through the window and you can see Santa!" I said that for a while and then I started saying, "Step on the Magic Star and you can see Cher!" And people got excited.

Some people in the other line, the line to sit on Santa's lap, went wild and cut through the gates so that they could stand on my Magic Star. Then they got angry when they looked through the Magic Window and saw Santa rather than Cher. What did they honestly expect? Is Cher so hard up for money that she'd agree to stand behind a two-way mirror at Macy's?

The angry people must have said something to management because I was taken off the Magic Star and sent to Elf Island, which is really boring as all you do is stand around and act merry. At noon a huge group of retarded people came to visit Santa and passed me on my little island. These people were profoundly retarded. They were rolling their eyes and wagging their tongues and staggering toward the Magic Tree. It was a large group of retarded people and after watching them for a few minutes I could not begin to guess where the retarded people ended and the regular New Yorkers began.

Everyone looks retarded once you set your mind to it.

All we sell in SantaLand are photos.

It is the SantaLand policy to take a picture of every child, which the parent can either order or refuse. People are allowed to bring their own cameras, video recorders, whatever. It is the multimedia groups that exhaust me. These are parents bent over with equipment, relentless in their quest for documentation.

During these visits the children are rarely allowed to discuss their desires with Santa. They are too busy being art-directed by the parents.

"All right, now let's get a shot of Anthony, Damascus, Theresa, Doug, Amy, Paul, *and* Vanity — can we squeeze them all together? Santa, how about you let Doug sit on your shoulders, can we do that?"

"Vanity and Damascus, look over here, no, look *here.*"

"Santa, can you put your arm around Amy and shake hands with Paul at the same time?"

"That's good. That's nice."

Sometimes the parent asks you to stand beside the child and wave. I do so. I stand beside a child and wave to the video camera wondering where I will wind up. I picture myself on the television set in a paneled room in Wapahanset or Easternmost Meadows. I picture the family fighting over command of the remote control, hitting the fast-forward button. The child's wave becomes a rapid salute. I enter the picture and everyone in the room entertains the same thought: "What's that asshole doing in our Christmas Memory tape?"

Young children, ages two to four, tend to be frightened of Santa. They have no interest in having their pictures taken because they don't know what a picture is. They're not vain, they're babies. They are babies and they act accordingly — they cry. A Photo Elf understands that, once a child starts crying, it's over.

The parents had planned to send the photos to relatives and place them in scrapbooks. They waited in line for over an hour and are not about to give up so easily. Tonight I saw a woman slap and shake her sobbing daughter, yelling, "Goddamn it, Rachel, get on that man's lap and smile or I'll give you something to cry about."

The mother shook her daughter until everyone's eyes were rolling in their heads. Then she sat Rachel on Santa's lap and I took the picture which supposedly means, on paper, that everything is snowy and wonderful.

It's not about the child or Santa or Christmas or anything but the parents' idea of a world they cannot make work for them.

VOICE OVER.   "The following elves are now excused for their afternoon breaks: Puff, Noel, Crumpet, Carol, Li'l Frosty, and Dreidel."

Our Elfin Guide says that we must cover our uniforms with a shirt or smock while dining in the cafeteria. It's funny that they would use the word "dining." Grown men and women in candy cane leggings do not dine. They feed. For the first week we had to suffer the jokes of the year-round employees who laughed at our costumes, not knowing that we make more money than they do.

Yesterday, I sat beside a Flushing elf named Gingersnap. She is a squat, plump woman whose knickers fit her like tights. Complementing the overall look is a thick pair of oversized glasses and a swarm of plastic barrettes she uses to clamp down her hair. I'd noticed Gingersnap back in training and am surprised she's lasted this long. No one can say she's not enthusiastic, any more spirit and they'd have to medicate her. Her problem is that she's, well, stupid. During training she had her hand in the air every two minutes, asking questions that were so obvious I wondered how she ever managed to find her way to the eighth floor.

We'd be running overtime, ready to go home, and she'd raise her hand and ask, "Can we wear our costumes home?" Who would want to? What possible pleasure could it give you to board the subway dressed as a gnome? The management had already laid down the law about our uniforms. Her question was pointless. It was like asking, "Can we force children onto Santa's lap at knife point?" Ummm.... No. The answer is no. Now if you could just sit down and shut up. At the end of our training session I watched her approach a manager asking if she could work as an elf year-round.

I've met elves from all walks of life. Most of them are show business people, actors and dancers, but a surprising number of them held real jobs at advertising agencies and brokerage firms before the recession hit. Bless their hearts, these people never imagined there was a velvet costume in their future. They're the really bitter elves.

I had lunch this afternoon with someone I've code named, "Flakey." She's recently moved here from Kansas City and is not very happy to be working for Santa. Every time I come upon her she's telling someone, "I'd rather be a starving artist in New York than to be artistically starving in Kansas City, Missouri." It makes me wince. She even says this to children. "I'm not a real elf, I'm an artist." Today she showed me some slides of her work. During her off hours Flakey stays busy gluing human hair to radios and telephone receivers. Everything she touches winds up looking like a Persian cat.

"Oh," I said, "What a cute idea." This was the wrong thing to say. She strenuously objected to the word, "cute," and then tried to sell me a blonde clock radio, telling me she'd be willing to let it go for $300. I said, "Aside from the fact that I don't have $300, who really wants to part the bangs of their alarm clock in order to read the time?"

So far, my least favorite elf is a guy from Florida whom I call "The Walrus." The Walrus has a handlebar mustache, no chin, and a neck the size of my waist. In the dressing room he confesses to being "a bit of a ladies' man."

The Walrus acts as though SantaLand were a single's bar. It is embarrassing to work with him. We'll be together at the Magic Window, where he pulls women aside, places his arm around their shoulders and says, "I know you're not going to ask Santa for good looks. You've already got those, pretty lady."

In his mind, the women are charmed, dizzy with his attention.

I pull him aside and say, "That was a *mother* you just did that to, a married woman with three children."

He says, "Hey man, I didn't see any ring." Then he turns to the next available woman and whistles, "Santa's married but I'm not."

But most of the elves are high school and college students. They're young and cute and one of the job perks is that I get to see them in their underpants. The changing rooms are located in the employee bathrooms behind SantaLand. The men's bathroom is small and the toilets often flood, so we are forced to stand on an island of newspapers to keep our socks

20

dry. The Santas have a nice dressing room across the hall, but you don't want to see a Santa undress.

The overall cutest elf is a fellow from Queens named Snowball. Snowball tends to ham it up with the children, sometimes literally tumbling down the path to Santa's house. I tend to frown on that sort of behavior but Snowball is hands down adorable — you want to put him in your pocket. Yesterday we worked together as Santa Elves and I became excited when he started saying things like, "I'd follow *you* to Santa's house any day, Crumpet." It made me dizzy, this flirtation.

By mid-afternoon I was running into walls. At the end of our shift we were in the bathroom, changing clothes, when suddenly we were surrounded by three Santas and five other elves — all of them were guys that Snowball had been flirting with.

Snowball just leads elves on, elves and Santas.

Later on we were in the elevator and I heard him say to his friend, "I don't know what these guys all want with me. It gives me the creeps the way they stare."

Snowball is playing a dangerous game. It's one thing to get a child fired up but you really don't want to be working under a jilted Santa.

VOICE OVER. "Breaking elves should now report to the manager's station for reassignment. Break is over."

At least a third of Santa's visitors are adults: couples, and a surprising number of men and women alone. Most of the single people don't want to sit on Santa's lap; they just stop by to shake his hand and wish him luck. Often the single adults are foreigners who just happened to be shopping at Macy's and got bullied into the Maze by the Entrance Elf, whose job it is to hustle people in. One moment the foreigner is looking at china, and the next thing he knows he is standing at the Magic Tree, where an elf holding a palm-sized counter asks, "How many in your party?"

The foreigner answers, "Yes."

"How many in your party is not a yes or no question."

"Yes."

Then a Santa Elf leads the way to a house where the confused and exhausted visitor addresses a bearded man in a red suit and says, "Yes, OK. Today I am good."

There was this one guy who came to visit Santa, a sloppy, good-looking man in his mid-forties. I thought he was another confused European, so I reassured him that many adults come to visit Santa, everyone is welcome. An hour later, I noticed the same man, back again to fellowship with Santa. I asked what he and Santa talk about, and in a cracked and puny voice he answered, "Toys. All the toys."

I noticed a dent in the left side of his forehead. You could place an acorn in a dent like this. He waited in line and returned to visit a third time. On his final visit he got so excited he peed on Santa's lap.

There were two New Jersey families who came together to see Santa. Two loud, ugly husbands with two wives and four children between them. The children gathered around Santa and had their picture taken. When Santa asked the ten-year-old boy what he wanted for Christmas, the father shouted, "A WOMAN! GET HIM A WOMAN, SANTA!" These men were very loud and irritating, constantly laughing and jostling one another. The two women sat on Santa's lap and had their picture taken and each asked for a KitchenAid brand dishwasher and a decent winter coat. The husbands sat on Santa's lap and, when asked what he wanted for Christmas, one of the men yelled, "I WANT A BROAD WITH BIG TITS!" The man's small-breasted wife crossed her arms over her chest, looked at the floor, and gritted her teeth. The man's son tried to laugh.

So far in SantaLand, I have seen the old Simone from *General Hospital*, Shawn from *All My Children*, Walter Cronkite, and Phil Collins. Last year one of the elves was suspended after asking Goldie Hawn to autograph her hand. We have been instructed to leave stars alone.

Phil Collins was small and well groomed. He arrived with his daughter and an entourage of three. I don't care about Phil Collins one way or the other but I saw some people who might and I felt it was my duty to tap them on the shoulder and say, "Look, there's Phil Collins!"

Many of Santa's visitors are from out of town and welcome the opportunity to view a celebrity, as it rounds out their New York experience. I'd point out Phil Collins and people would literally squeal with delight. Seeing as it is my job to make people happy, I don't have any problem with it. Phil Collins wandered through the Maze, videotaping everything with his camcorder and enjoying himself. Once he entered the Magic Tree, he was no longer visible to the Maze audience, so I began telling people that if they left immediately and took a right at the end of the hall, they could probably catch up with Phil Collins after his visit with Santa. So they did. People left. When Phil Collins walked out of SantaLand, there was a crowd of fifty to sixty people waiting for autographs. When the managers came looking for the big mouth, I said, "Phil Collins, who's he?"

But what's really exciting is I was talking with Sleighbell, an entertainer who is in the process of making a music video with her all-girl singing group. We talked about one thing and another, and she told me that she has appeared on a few tele-

23

vision shows, mainly soap operas. I asked if she has ever done *One Life To Live*, and she said, yes, she had a bit part as a flamenco dancer a few years ago when Cord and Tina married and traveled to Madrid for their honeymoon.

Suddenly I remembered Sleighbell perfectly. I remember Cord and Tina's honeymoon like it was yesterday. On that episode she wore a red lace dress and stomped upon a shiny nightclub floor until Spain's greatest bullfighter entered, challenging Cord to a duel. Sleighbell intervened. She stopped dancing and said to Cord, "Don't do it, Señor. Yout be a fool to fight weeth Spain's greatest boolfighter!"

Anyway, we were talking when Carlton, another manager, got involved and said that he'd been on *One Life To Live* seven times. He played Clint's lawyer five years ago when the entire Buchanan family was on trial for the murder of Mitch Laurence. Carlton knows Victoria Buchanan personally and said that she's just as sweet and caring in real life as she is on the show.

"She's basically playing herself, except for the multiple personality disorder."

Carlton told me that Clint tends to keep to himself but that Bo and Asa are a lot of fun. I can't believe I'm hearing these things. I know people who have sat around with Tina, Cord, Nicki, Asa, and Clint. I'm honing in. I'm getting closer, I can feel it.

All the Santas have different routines. Some want the children's names. So as you are leading the youngsters from the Magic Tree you say, "What was your name again? It's right on the tip of my mind where I can't get at it."

Then they say their name and you say, "That's right. Van."

You lead them to Santa's door and say, "Let me just check

to see if he's ready." And you poke your head in and whisper, "Van!"

Then half the time you'll usher the child into the house and Santa will say, "Stan! It's so good to see you!"

It's hard to keep the names straight and some of the names are names I've never heard — Vaneesha, Fohntaj, Great. A child names Great. "I'm Great!" That's a name which is bound to prove challenging once he gets old enough to start sleeping around.

Santa Howard uses names and sits the kids on his lap and asks if they've been good and what they want for Christmas, and then asks what they plan to leave him on Christmas Eve and they say "cookies and milk" and he asks " What kind of cookies?" and they say "chocolate chip" or whatever and he demands that the photo elf say "Chocolate chip! That's Santa's favorite kind of cookie." I don't mind saying it, but I must have said it sixty times today.

Then in the afternoon Santa Howard got an Asian child who wasn't familiar with the idea of leaving cookies. Santa asked what she was going to leave him to eat and she got a puzzled look on her face. He said, "Something round to eat?" And she said, "A potato?"

I hate working with Santa Doug who tends to spit when he talks. It just gushes out, every time he opens his mouth. Tonight a little girl wiped her face asking, "Santa, why are you spitting on me?" Doug explained that it wasn't spit, it was simply frost coming off his beard. That might work on a six-year-old but what does he tell his friends?

The worst is Santa Santa. I don't know his real name; no one does. During most days, there is a slow period when you sit around the house and talk to your Santa. Most of them are nice guys and we sit around and laugh, but Santa Santa takes himself a bit too seriously. I asked him where he lives, Brooklyn or Manhattan, and he said, "Why, I live at the North Pole with Mrs. Claus!" I asked what he does the rest of the year and he said, "I make toys for all of the children."

I was like, "Yeah, but what do you do for money?"

"Santa doesn't need money," he said.

Santa Santa sits and waves and jingles his bell sash when no one is there. He actually recited "The Night Before Christmas," and it was just the two of us in the house, no children. Just us. What do you do with a nut like that?

He says, "Oh, Little Elf, Little Elf, bring Santa a throat lozenge." I reminded him that I have a name, Crumpet, and then I brought him a lozenge.

Santa Santa has an elaborate little act for the children. He'll talk to them and give a hearty chuckle and ring his bells and then he asks them to name their favorite Christmas carol. Most of them say, "Rudolph, the Red-Nosed Reindeer." Santa Santa then asks if they will sing it for him. The children are shy and don't want to sing out loud, so Santa Santa says, "Oh, Little Elf, Little Elf! Help young Brenda to sing that favorite carol of hers." Then I have to stand there and sing "Rudolph, the Red-Nosed Reindeer," which I hate. Then late in the afternoon, a child said she didn't know what her favorite Christmas carol was. Santa Santa suggested, "Away in the Manger." The little girl agreed to it but didn't want to sing it because she didn't know the words.

Santa Santa said, "Oh, Little Elf, Little Elf, come sing 'Away in the Manger' for us."

It didn't seem fair that I should have to solo, so I told him I didn't know the words.

Santa Santa said, "Of course you know the words. Come now, sing!"

So I sang it the way Billie Holiday might have sung it if she'd put out a Christmas album. "Away in the manger, no crib for a bed, the little Lord, Jesus, lay down his sweet head."

Santa Santa did not allow me to finish.

Out of all the Santas, two are black and both are so light skinned that, with the beard and makeup, you would be hard-pressed to determine their race.

Last week, a black woman became upset when, having requested a "Santa of color," she was sent to Jerome.

"He's not black," the woman complained.

We assured this woman that Jerome was indeed black.

The woman said, "Well, he isn't black enough."

Jerome is a difficult Santa, moody and unpredictable. He spends a lot of time staring off into space and tallying up his paycheck for the hours he has worked so far. Jerome seems to have his own bizarre agenda. When the children arrive, he looks down at his boots and lectures them, suggesting a career in entomology.

He tells them that the defensive spray of the stink bug may contain medicinal powers that can one day cure mankind of communicable diseases.

"Do you know about holistic medicine?" he asks.

The Photo Elf takes a picture of yawning children.

The last time I was the Pointer Elf, a woman approached me and whispered, "We would like a *traditional* Santa. I'm sure you know what I'm talking about." I sent her to Jerome.

A man pulled Snowball aside, saying, "Last year we were stuck with a chocolate Santa. Make sure it doesn't happen again."

Today, I was Pointer Elf for all of five minutes before a woman touched my arm and mouthed, "White — white like *us.*"

27

I've had requests from both sides. White Santa, black Santa, a Pointer Elf is instructed to shrug his shoulders and feign ignorance, saying, "There's only one Santa."

Today I worked as an Exit Elf, telling people in a loud voice, "THIS WAY OUT OF SANTALAND." A woman was standing at one of the cash registers paying for her pictures, while her son lay beneath her, kicking and heaving, having a tantrum. The woman said, "Riley, if you don't start behaving yourself, Santa's not going to bring you *any* of those toys you asked for."

The child said, "He is too going to bring me the toys, liar, he already told me."

The woman grabbed my arm and said, "You there, Elf, tell Riley here that if he doesn't start behaving immediately, then Santa's going to change his mind and bring him coal for Christmas."

I said that Santa no longer traffics in coal. Instead, if you're bad he comes to your house and steals things. I told Riley that if he didn't behave himself, Santa was going to take away his TV and all his electrical appliances and leave him in the dark. "All your appliances, including the refrigerator. Your food is going to spoil and smell bad. It's going to be so cold and dark where you are. Man, Riley, are you ever going to suffer. You're going to wish you never heard the name Santa."

The woman got a worried look on her face and said, "All right, that's enough."

I said, "He's going to take your car and your furniture and all the towels and blankets and leave you with nothing."

The woman said, "No, that's enough, really."

Have you ever realized that *Santa* is an anagram of *Satan*. I imagined a SatanLand where visitors would wade through steaming pools of human blood and feces before arriving at the Gates of Hell, where a hideous imp in a singed velvet costume would take them by the hand and lead them toward Satan. Once I thought of it I couldn't get it out of my mind. Overhearing the customers I would substitute the word *Satan* for the word *Santa*.

"What do you think, Michael? Do you think Macy's has the real Satan?"

"Don't forget to thank Satan for the Baby Alive he got you last year."

"I love Satan."

"Who doesn't? Everybody loves Satan."

Father Christmas or the Devil — so close but yet so far.

VOICE OVER. "Attention Macy's shoppers." *(Jingle, jingle.)* "Remember that you've got only twelve shopping days left before Christmas."

As Christmas approaches we grow progressively busier. There is no longer any down time and I think they need to outfit all the elves with cans of mace. It's all Santa, Santa, Santa. Not even the children have respect for elves unless it's the dwarf and then, "Oh!," they go wild. Everybody wants their picture taken with that goddamned dwarf. Physically, she looks the part, sure, but if you ask me, she's just coasting on her looks.

I got a new haircut today and a few people complimented me but it didn't register. I spend all day lying to people, saying, "You look so pretty," and, "Santa can't wait to visit with you. You're all he talks about. It's just not Christmas without you. You're Santa's favorite person in the entire tri-state area." Sometimes I lay it on real thick: "Aren't you the princess of Rongovia? Santa said a beautiful Princess was coming here to visit him. He said she would be wearing a red dress and that she was very pretty, but not stuck up or two-faced. That's you, isn't it?" I lay it on and the parents mouth the words "Thank you" and "Good job."

To one child I said, "You're a model, aren't you?" The girl was maybe six years old and said, "Yes, I model, but I also act. I just got a second call-back for a Fisher Price commercial." The girl's mother said, "You may recognize Katelyn from the 'My First Sony' campaign. She's on the box." I said yes, of course.

All I do is lie, and that has made me immune to compliments. I think I'm starting to lose it.

VOICE OVER. "Attention holiday shoppers. Remember that there are only nine more days before Christmas."

I changed my elf name from Crumpet to Blisters. It's a little on the trollish side but circumstances have eroded my elfin spirit. I was with Santa Carl when a mother came in with her child saying, "All right, Jason. Tell Santa what you want. Tell him what you want."

Jason said, "I want ... Procton and ... Gamble to ... stop animal testing." The mother rapped her son over the head saying, "Proctor. That's Proctor and Gamble. And what do they do to animals? Do they torture animals, Jason? Is that what they do?"

Jason said, "Yes, they torture." He was maybe six years old.

Then later, I was working as a Counter Elf at the Magic Tree when I saw a woman unzip her son's fly and instruct him to pee into a bank of artificial snow. He was a young child, four or five years old, and he did it, he peed. SantaLand might *look* like the outdoors but on careful inspection you can't help but notice four walls and a ceiling.

VOICE OVER. "Attention everyone, from your friends at Macy's. Remember that you have only seven more shopping days until Christmas."

Today a child told Santa Ken that he wanted his dead father back and a complete set of Teenage Mutant Ninja Turtles. Everyone wants those Turtles.

VOICE OVER. "Look, people, you've only got three more days to shop for Christmas."

I manned the "Oh My God" Corner. We were packed, absolutely packed and everyone seemed to stop me with a question.

"Which way to the down escalator — which way to the elevator — The Patio Restaurant — gift wrap — Trim-A-Tree." There was a line for Santa and a line for the women's bathroom and one woman, having asked me a thousand questions already, got up in my face asking, "Which is the line for the women's bathroom?" I shouted that I thought it was the line with all the women in it. Then she said, "I'm going to have you fired."

I had two people say that to me today, "I'm going to have you fired." Go ahead, be my guest. I'm wearing a green velvet costume; it doesn't get any worse than this. Who do these people think they are?

"I'm going to have you fired," and I wanted to lean over and say, "I'm going to have you killed."

VOICE OVER. "This is just a reminder that Macy's *will be closed* on Christmas Day. This leaves you with one more shopping day. That's it. One."

31

This was my last day of work. We'd been told that Christmas eve would be slow but this was the busiest I'd ever seen it, the chaos a week's worth of training had prepared us for — twenty-three thousand desperate people behaving as though they were trying to board the last train out of town. I started at the Magic Tree where I witnessed a fist fight between two mothers. I watched as a woman experienced a severe, crowd-related anxiety attack. Falling to the filthy floor she groped for breath, her arms moving as if she was fighting off bats. Parents in long lines tossed disposable diapers into the Candy Cane Forest and offered cash bribes to cut in line. A Long Island father called Santa a faggot when he refused to recite "The Night Before Christmas" to his child and, through it all, the noise was deafening with children crying and parents shouting, "What more do you want me to do? We're *here*, all right? Now shut up." This was the rowdiest crowd I'd ever seen and we were short on elves, many of whom waited until the last minute to show their true colors: calling in sick or simply not showing up. Many elves complained but the rest of us found ourselves in the moment we'd been waiting for. It was us against them, time to be a trooper and I surrendered completely.

I was sent to Santa Randy who had them on the lap, and off the lap in thirty seconds flat. He was like one of those talking dolls equipped with no more than six simple phrases.

"I know what you want for Christmas. There's no need to even tell me because Santa knows everything. Ready for a picture? Goodness, that was fun. All right then, see you next year."

His lap would still be warm from the last child and he'd turn to me saying, "I deserve an affair, Goddamnit it. Nothing life threatening, just something to hold me over for the next few years." Children would be waiting at the door and he'd snap out of it, saying, "I know what you want for Christmas. There's no need to even tell me because Santa knows every-

32

thing. Hey, how's about a picture? Goodness that was fun. All right then, see you next year."

When his shift ended, Randy was replaced by a Santa I'd never worked with before. Usually the guy's name is written on the water cups they keep hidden on the toy shelf. I looked on the cup and saw no name. It was early evening and we were too busy to pause for an introduction. Noting a group of visitors huddled upon his doorstep, my Santa began to sing, "A pretty girl ... is like a melody."

The parents and children entered the room and, noting the young girl, Santa held his gloved hand to his chest and fell back upon his cushion, faking a massive heart attack. He moaned for a few moments before saying, "Elf, Elf ... are you there?'

"Yes, Santa, I'm here."

"Elf, I just had a dream that I was seated before the most beautiful girl in the world. She was right here, in my house."

Then I say, "It wasn't a dream, Santa. Open your eyes, my friend. She's standing before you right this moment."

Santa rubbed his eyes, "Oh, heavenly day," he said, "You are *the* most beautiful girl I have seen in six hundred and seventeen years."

The he scooped her up into his lap and flattered every aspect of her character. The child was delirious, the center of attention. Santa then gestured toward the child's mother, asking, "Is that your sister I see standing in the corner?"

"No, that's my mother, silly."

Santa called the woman close and asked if she had been a good mother. "Do you tell your daughter that you love her? Do you tell her every day?"

The mothers blushed saying, "I try, Santa."

"And you, Sir, step forward." The father shuffled to Santa's feet. "What do you do besides make money? If I were lucky enough to have young Kathleen as my daughter I'd kiss her forehead ten times a day and thank her for bringing such joy into my life. Let me see you do that. It would mean a lot to me." The father kissed his daughter's forehead.

Santa ended the visit saying, "Remember that the most important thing is to try and love other people as much as they love you."

The great thing about this Santa is that he never even asked what the children wanted. He tailored his reception to each specific group. The main thing was that he made them feel welcome and relaxed enough to drop their guard and submit to his idea of Christmas. Me, I can go any old way. If you want to hustle them along then I will be your sheepdog, herding them in one door and out the other. If you want to make fun of them I'm one step ahead of you. This though, it threw me completely because I'm not a good person and never have been. Before this evening I'd never even been accidentally mistaken for a good person but suddenly I was good by association. Families left grabbing my hands and thanking me. These were grown men and women, crying like babies on the night before Christmas.

My plane was set to leave at eight o'clock and I stayed until the very last moment. It was with reservation that I reported to the manager, telling her I had to leave. And oh, suddenly I loved this woman. She's raised her voice a few times but her anger had been directed at the *old* me. I felt certain she would recognize the change and together we would share a special moment. Maybe we'd cry for a moment or two and surely I'd be left with the kind of warmth a person can hold in their hearts forever. I'd stuck it out and expected she might want to place my cap in the elfin hall of fame.

I searched the room and joined her behind the counter where she was talking to a customer. I touched her arm and said, "I have to go now." She laid her hand on my shoulder, squeezed it gently, and continued her conversation, saying, "Don't tell the store manager I called you a bitch, tell him I called you a fucking bitch, because that's exactly what you are. Now get out of my sight before I do something we both regret."

The customer fled.

And me, I was one step ahead of her.

SEASON'S GREETINGS TO OUR FRIENDS AND FAMILY!!!

SEASON'S GREETINGS TO
OUR FRIENDS AND FAMILY!!!

Many of you, our friends and family, are probably taken aback by this, our annual holiday newsletter. You've read of our recent tragedy in the newspapers and were no doubt thinking that, what with all of their sudden legal woes and "hassles," the Dunbar clan might just stick their heads in the sand and avoid this upcoming holiday season altogether!!

You're saying, "There's no way the Dunbar family can grieve their terrible loss *and* carry on the traditions of the season. No family is *that* strong," you're thinking to yourselves.

Well, think again!!!!!!!!!!!!

While this past year has certainly dealt our family a heavy hand of sorrow and tribulation, we have (so far!) weathered the storm and shall continue to do so! Our tree is standing tall in the living room, the stockings are hung, and we are eagerly awaiting the arrival of a certain portly gentleman who goes by the name "Saint Nick"!!!!!!!!!!!!

Our trusty PC printed out our wish lists weeks ago and now we're cranking it up again to wish you and yours The Merriest of Christmas Seasons from the entire Dunbar family: Clifford, Jocelyn, Kevin, Jacki, Kyle, and Khe Sahn!!!!!

Some of you are probably reading this and scratching your heads over the name "Khe Sahn." "That certainly doesn't fit with he rest of the family names," you're saying to yourself. "What, did those crazy Dunbars get themselves a Siamese cat?" You're close.

To those of you who live in a cave and haven't heard the

39

news, allow us to introduce Khe Sahn Dunbar who, at the age of twenty-two happens to be the newest member of our family.

Surprised?

JOIN THE CLUB!!!!!!!

It appears that Clifford, husband of yours truly and father to our three natural children, accidentally planted the seeds for Khe Sahn twenty-two years ago during his stint in ... where else?

VIETNAM!!!! *Sushi (sense memory recall)*

Clifford Dunbar, twenty-two years ago, a young man in a war-torn country, made a mistake, A terrible, heinous mistake. A stupid, thoughtless, permanent mistake with dreadful, haunting consequences.

But who are you, who are any of us, to judge him for it? Especially now, with Christmas at our heels. Who are we to judge?

When his tour of duty ended Clifford returned home, where he and I were reunited. We lived, you might remember, in that tiny apartment over on Halsey Street. Clifford had just begun his satisfying career at Sampson Interlock and I was working part-time, accounting for Hershel Beck when ... along came the children!!!!!! We struggled and saved and eventually (finally!!) bought our house on Tiffany Circle, number 714, where the Dunbar clan remains nested to this very day!!!!

It was here, 714 Tiffany Circle, where I first encountered Khe Sahn, who arrived at our door on (as fate would have it) Halloween!!!

I recall mistaking her for a Trick-or-Treater! She wore, I remember, a skirt the size of a beer cozy, a short, furry jacket, and, on her face, enough rouge, eye shadow, and lipstick to paint our entire house, inside and out. She's a very small person and I mistook her for a child, a child masquerading as a prostitute. I handed her a fistful of chocolate nougats, hoping that, like the other children, she would quickly move on to the next house.

But Khe Sahn was no Trick-or-Treater.

I started to close the door but was interrupted by her interpreter, a very feminine-looking man carrying an attaché case. He introduced himself in English and then turned to Khe Sahn, speaking a language I have sadly come to recognize as Vietnamese. While our language flows from our mouths, the Vietnamese language sounds as though it is being forced from the speaker by a series of heavy and merciless blows to the stomach. The words themselves are the sounds of pain. Khe Sahn responded to the interpreter, her voice as high-pitched and relentless as a car alarm. The two of them stood on my doorstep screeching away in Vietnamese while I stood by, frightened and confused.

I am still, to this day, frightened and confused. Very much so. It is frightening that, after all this time, a full-grown bastard (I use that word technically) can cross the seas and make herself comfortable in my home, all with the blessing of our government. Twenty-two years ago Uncle Sam couldn't stand the Vietnamese. Now he's dressing them like prostitutes and moving them into our houses!!!! Out of nowhere this young woman has entered our lives with the force and mystery of the Swine Flu and there appears to be nothing we can do about it. Out of nowhere this land mine knocks upon our door and we are expected to recognize her as our child!!!!??????????

Clifford likes to say that the Dunbar children inherited their mother's looks and their father's brains. It's true: Kevin, Jackelyn, and Kyle are all just as good-looking as they can possibly be! And smart? Well, they're smart enough, smart like their father, with the exception of our oldest son Kevin. After graduating Moody High with honors, Kevin is currently enrolled in his third year at Feeny State, majoring in chemical engineering. He's made the honor roll every semester and there seems to be no stopping him!!! A year and a half left to go and already the job offers are pouring in!

We love you, Kevin!!!!!!!!!!!!!!!!!!!

We sometimes like to joke that when God handed out brains to the Dunbar kids He saw Kevin standing first in line and awarded him the whole sack!!! What the other children lack in brains they seem to make up for in one way or another. They have qualities and personalities and make observations, unlike Khe Sahn, who seems to believe she can coast through life on her looks alone!! She hasn't got the ambition God gave a sparrow! She arrived in this house six weeks ago speaking only the words "Daddy," "Shiny," and "Five dollar now."

Quite a vocabulary!!!!!!!!!!

While an industrious person might buckle down and seriously study the language of her newly adopted country, Khe Sahn appeared to be in no hurry whatsoever. When asked a simple question such as, "Why don't you go back where you came from?" she would touch my hand and launch into a spasm of Vietnamese drivel — as if I were the outsider, expected to learn *her* language! We were visited several times by Lonnie Tipit, that "interpreter," that "man" who accompanied Khe Sahn on her first visit. Mr. Tipit seemed to feel that the Dunbar door was open for him anytime, day or night. He'd drop by (most often during the supper hours) and, between helpings of *my* home-cooked meals (thank you very much), "touch base" with his "friend," Khe Sahn. "I don't think she's getting enough exposure to the community," he would say. "Why don't you start taking her around town, to church get-togethers and local events?" Well, that was easy for *him* to say! I told him, I said, "*You* try taking a girl in a halter top to a confirmation class. *You* take her to the Autumn Craft Caravan and watch her snatch every shiny object that catches her eye. I've learned my lesson already."

Lonnie Tipit went so far as to suggest that we hire him as Khe Sahn's English tutor at, get this, seventeen dollars an hour!!!!!!!!!!! Seventeen dollars an hour so she can learn to lisp and twitter and flutter her hands like two small birds? NO, THANK YOU!!!!!!!

I am not in the habit of throwing my money away. And that, my friends, is what it would have amounted to. A person has to *want* to learn. I know that. Apparently, back in Ho Chi Minh City, Her Majesty was treated like a queen and sees no reason to change her ways!!!! Her Highness rises at around noon, wolfs down a fish or two (all she eats is fish and chicken breasts), and settles herself before the makeup mirror, waiting for her father to return home from work. At the sound of his car in the driveway she perks up and races to the door like a spaniel, panting and wagging her tail to beat the band! Suddenly she is eager to please and attempt conversation!! Well, I don't know how they behave in Vietnam, but in the United States it is not customary for a half-dressed daughter to offer her father a five-dollar massage!!!

After having spent an exhausting day attempting to communicate a list of simple chores, I would stand in amazement at Khe Sahn's sudden grasp of English when faced with my husband.

"Daddy happy five dollar shiny now, OK?"

"You big feet friendly with ABC Khe Sahn. You Big Bird Daddy Grover."

Apparently she had picked up a few words while watching "Sesame Street."

"Daddy special special funky fresh jam party commercial free jam."

43

She began listening to the radio.

Khe Sahn treats our youngest son, Kyle, with complete indifference, which is probably a blessing in disguise. This entire episode has been very difficult for Kyle, who, at age fifteen, tends to be the artistic loner of the family. He keeps to himself, spending many hours in his bedroom, where he burns incense, listens to music, and carves gnomes out of soap. Kyle is very good-looking and talented and we are looking forward to the day when he sets aside his jackknife and bar of Irish Spring and begins "carving out" a future rather than a shriveled troll! He is at that very difficult age but we pray he will grow out of it and follow his brother's footsteps to success before it is too late. Hopefully, the disasters of his sister, Jackelyn, will open his eyes to the hazards of drugs, the calamity of a thoughtless, premature marriage, and the heartaches of parenthood!

We had, of course, warned our daughter against marrying Timothy Speaks. We warned, threatened, cautioned, advised, what have you — but it did no good as a young girl, with all the evidence before her, sees only what she *wants* to see. The marriage was bad enough but the news of her pregnancy struck her father and me with the force of a hurricane.

Timothy Speaks, the father of our grandchild? How could it be????

Timothy Speaks, who had his back and neck tattooed with brilliant flames. His neck!!!

We told Jacki, "One of these days he's going to have to grow up and find a job, and when he does, those employers are going to wonder why he's wearing a turtleneck under his business suit. People with tattooed necks do not, as a rule, hold down high-paying jobs," we said.

She ran back to Timothy repeating our warning…. Lo and behold, two days later, *she* showed up with a tattooed neck as

well!!!!! They even made plans to have their baby tattooed!!!!
A tattoo, on an infant!!!!!!!!!!!!

Timothy Speaks held our daughter in a web of madness that threatened to ensnare the entire Dunbar family.

The Jackelyn Dunbar-Speaks who lived with Timothy in that squalid "space" on West Vericose Avenue bore no resemblance to the beautiful girl pictured in our photo albums. The sensitive and considerate daughter we once knew became, under his fierce coaching, a mean-spirited, unreliable, and pregnant ghost who eventually gave birth to a ticking time bomb!!!!!

We, of course, saw it coming. The child, born September tenth under the influence of drugs, spent the first two months of his life in the critical care unit of St. Joe's Hospital. (At a whopping cost and guess who paid the bill for *that* one?) Faced with the concrete responsibility of fatherhood, Timothy Speaks abandoned his sick wife and child. Gone. Poof!

Surprised?

We saw it coming and are happy to report that, as of this writing, we have no idea where he is or what he is up to. (We could guess, but why bother?)

We have all read the studies and understand that a drug-addicted baby faces a difficult, uphill battle in terms of living a normal life. This child, having been given the legal name "Satan Speaks" would, we felt, have a harder time than most. We were lucky enough to get Jacki into a fine treatment center on the condition that the child remain here with us until which time (if ever) she is able to assume responsibility for him. The child arrived at our home on November tenth and shortly thereafter, following her initial withdrawal, Jacki granted us permission to address it as "Don." Don, a nice, simple name.

It made a difference, believe me.

While I could not describe him as being a "normal" baby, taking care of young Don gave me a great deal of pleasure. Terribly insistent, prone to hideous rashes, a twenty-four-hour round-the-clock screamer, he was our grandchild and we loved him. Knowing that he would physically grow to adulthood while maintaining the attention span of a common housefly did not, in the least bit, diminish our feelings for him.

Clifford would sometimes joke that Don was a "Crack Baby" because he woke us at the crack of dawn!

I would then take the opportunity to mention that Khe Sahn was something of a "Crack Baby" herself, wandering around our house all hours of the day and night wearing nothing but a pair of hot pants and a glorified sports bra. Most nights, the dinnertime napkin in her lap provided more coverage than she was accustomed to!!! Clifford suggested that I buy her a few decent dresses and a couple pairs of jeans and I tried, oh, how I tried! I sat with her, leafing through catalogs, and watched as she pawed the expensive designer outfits. I walked with her through Cut Throat's and Discount Plus and watched as she turned up her nose at their sensibly priced clothing. I don't know about you, but in *this* family the children are rewarded for hard work. Call me old-fashioned but if you want a fifty-dollar sweater you have to prove that you deserve it! If I've said it once I've said it a thousand times: "A family is not a charitable organization." Khe Sahn wanted something for nothing and I buttoned up my purse and said the most difficult word a parent can say, "No!" I made her several outfits, sewed them with my own hands, two floor-length dress, beautiful burlap dresses, but did she wear them? Of course not!!!

When the winter winds began to blow she took to draping herself in a bed blanket, huddling beside the fireplace. While her "Poor Little Match Girl" routine might win a Tony Award on Broadway it did nothing for this ticket holder!

46

She carried on, following at Clifford's heels, until Thanksgiving Day, when she was introduced to our son Kevin, home for the holiday. One look at Kevin and it was "Clifford? Clifford who?" as far as Khe Sahn was concerned. One look at our handsome son and the "Shivering Victim" dropped her blanket and showed her true colors. It is a fact that she appeared at our Thanksgiving table wearing nothing but a string bikini!!!!!!!!!!

"Not in *my* house," said yours truly! When I demanded she change into one of the dresses I had sewn for her, Khe Sahn frowned into her cranberry sauce, pretending not to understand. Clifford and Kevin tried to convince me that, in Vietnam, it is customary for the women to wear swimsuits on Thanksgiving Day but I still don't believe a word of it. Since when do the Vietnamese observe Thanksgiving? What do those people have to be thankful for? S.F.

She ruined our holiday dinner with her giggling, coy games. She sat beside Kevin until, insisting she had seen a spider in her chair, she moved into his lap!! "You new funky master jam party mix silly fresh spider five dollar Big Bird."

Those of you who know Kevin understand that, while he is an absolute whip at some things, he is terribly naive at others. Tall and good-looking, easy with a smile and a kind word, Kevin has been the target of many a huntress. Always the gentleman, he treated the young ladies like glass, which, looking back, was appropriate because you could see through each and every one of them. When he asked to bring a date home for Thanksgiving I said I thought it was a bad idea as we were all under more than enough stress already. Looking back, I wish he *had* brought a date, as it might have dampened the sky-high hopes and aspirations of Khe Sahn, his half-sister!!!!!!!!!!!

"Me no big big potato spoon fort tomorrow? Kevin have big big shiny face like hand of chicken soon with funky crazy Sesame Street jammy jam."

47

I could barely choke down my meal and found myself counting the minutes before Kevin, the greatest joy of our lives, called an end to the private English lesson he gave Khe Sahn in her bedroom, got into his car, and returned to Feeny State.

As I mentioned before, Kevin has always been a very caring person, always going out of his way to lend a hand or comfort a stranger. Being as that is his nature, he returned to school and, evidently, began phoning Khe Sahn, sometimes speaking with the aid of a Vietnamese student who acted as an interpreter. He was, in his own was, foolishly trying to make her feel welcome and adjust to life in her new, highly advanced country. That is the Kevin we all know and love, always trying to help a person less intelligent than himself, bending over backwards to coax a smile!

Unfortunately, Khe Sahn misinterpreted his interest as a declaration of romantic concern. She took to "manning" the telephone twenty-four hours a day, hovering above it and regarding it as though it were a living creature. Whenever (God forbid!) someone called for Clifford, Kyle, or me, she would simply hang up!!!!

Eventually, recognizing that her behavior bordered on madness, I had a word with her.

"HE'S NOT FOR YOU," I yelled. (I have been criticized for yelling, told that it doesn't serve any real purpose when speaking to a foreigner, but at least it gets their attention!) "HE'S MY SON IN COLLEGE. MY SON ON THE DEAN'S LIST, NOT FOR YOU."

She was perched beside the telephone with a curling iron in her hand. At the sound of my voice she instinctively turned her attention elsewhere.

"BOTH MY SON AND MY HUSBAND ARE OFF-LIMITS AS FAR AS YOU'RE CONCERNED, DO YOU UNDERSTAND? THEY ARE EACH RELATED TO YOU IN ONE WAY OR AN-

48

OTHER AND THAT MAKES IT WRONG. AUTOMATICALLY WRONG. BAD, BAD, WRONG! WRONG AND BAD TOGETHER FOR THE KHE SAHN TO BE WITH JOCELYN'S SON OR HUSBAND. BAD AND WRONG. DO YOU UNDERSTAND WHAT I AM SAYING NOW?"

She looked up for a moment or two before returning her attention to the electrical cord.

I gave up. Trying to explain moral principles to Khe Sahn was like reviewing a standard 1040 tax form with a house cat! She understands only what she chooses to understand. Say the word "shopping" and, quicker than you can blink, she's sitting in the front seat of the car! Try a more complicated word such as "sweep" or "iron" and she shrugs her shoulders and retreats to the bedroom.

Looking back, I suppose I had no valid reason to trust her sudden willingness to lend a hand but, on the day in question, I was nearing the end of my rope.

We were approaching Christmas, December sixteenth, when I made the thoughtless mistake of asking her to watch the child while I ran some errands. With a needy, shriveled newborn baby, a teenaged son, and a twenty-two-year-old, half-dressed "step-daughter" in my house, my hands were full from one moment to the next, twenty-eight hours a day!!!! It was nine days before Christmas and, busy as I was, I hadn't bought a single gift. (Santa, where are you????????)

On that early afternoon Kyle was in school, Clifford was at the office, and Khe Sahn was seated beside the telephone, picking at a leftover baked fish with her bare hands.

"WATCH THE BABY," I said. "WATCH DON, THE BABY, WHILE I GO OUT."

She considered her greasy fingers.

"YOU WATCH BABY DON WHILE JOCELYN GOES SHOPPING FOR SPECIAL PRESENT FOR THE KHE SAHN!"

I said. "HO, HO, HO, SPECIAL CHRISTMAS FOR THE KHE SAHN. HO, HO!"

At the mention of the word "shopping" she perked up and gave me her full attention. Having heard the radio and watched TV, she understood Christmas as an opportunity to receive gifts and was in the habit of poring over the mail-order catalogs and expressing her desires with the words "Ho, Ho, Ho."

I clearly remember my choice of words on that cold and cloudy December afternoon. I did not say "baby-sit," fearing that she might take me at my word and literally sit upon the baby.

"WATCH THE BABY," I said to that twenty-two-year-old adult on the afternoon of December sixteenth.

"WATCH THE BABY," I repeated as we stood over the crib and observed the wailing infant. I picked him up and rocked him gently as he struggled in my arms. "WATCH BABY."

"Watch Baby," Khe Sahn responded, holding out her arms to accept him. "Watch Baby for Jocelyn get shop special HO, HO, Ho, Khe Sahn fresh shiny."

"Exactly," I said, laying a hand on her shoulder.

I was, at that moment in time, convinced of her sincerity. I was big enough to set aside all of the trouble she had visited upon our household and give her another chance! "That is all behind us now," I said to myself, watching her cradle the wailing child.

Oh, what a fool I was!!!!!!!!!!!!!

Leaving the house and driving toward White Paw Center I felt a sense of relief I had not known in quite a while. This was the first time in weeks I had allowed myself a moment alone and, with six Dunbar wish lists burning a hole in my pocket, I intended to make the most of it!!!

I can't account for every moment of my afternoon. Never did it occur to me that I would one day be called upon to do so but, that being the case, I will report what I remember. I can comfortably testify that, on the afternoon of December sixteenth, I visited the White Paw Shopping Center, where I spent a brief amount of time in The Slack Heap, searching for a gift for Kyle. I found what he wanted but not in his size. I then left The Slack Heap and walked over to ____&____, where I bought a ____ for my daughter Jacki. (I'm not going to ruin anyone's Christmas surprises here. Why should I?) I stuck my head inside Turtleneck Crossing and searched for candles at Wax and Wane and I suppose I browsed. There are close to a hundred shops at the White Paw Center and you'll have to forgive me if I can't provide a detailed list of how long I spent in this or that store. I shopped until I grew wary of the time. It was getting dark, perhaps four-thirty, when I pulled into the driveway of our home on Tiffany Circle. I collected my packages from the car and entered my home, where I was immediately struck by the eerie silence. "This doesn't feel right to me," I remember saying to myself. It was an intuition, a mother's intuition.

"Something is wrong," I said to myself. "Something is terribly, terribly wrong."

Before calling out for Khe Sahn or checking on the baby I instinctively phoned the police. I then stood there, stock-still in the living room, staring at my shopping bags until they arrived (twenty-seven minutes later!!).

At the sound of the squad car in the driveway, Khe Sahn made an entrance, parading down the stairs in a black lace half-slip and a choker made from the cuff of Kevin's old choir robe.

"WHERE IS THE BABY?" I asked her. "WHERE IS DON?"

Accompanied by the police we went upstairs into the nursery and stood beside the empty crib.

"WHERE IS MY GRANDCHILD, DON? WHAT HAVE YOU DONE TO THE BABY?"

51

Khe Sahn, of course, said nothing. It is part of her act to tug at her hem line and feign shyness when first confronted by strangers. We left her standing there while the police and I began our search. We combed the entire house, the officers and I, before finally finding the helpless baby in the laundry room, warm but lifeless in the dryer.

The autopsy later revealed that Don had also been subjected to a wash cycle — hot wash, cold rinse. He died long before the spin cycle, which is, I suppose, the only blessing to be had in this entire ugly episode. I am still, to this day, haunted by the mental picture of my grandchild undergoing such brutality. The relentless pounding he received during his forty-five minutes in the dryer is something I would rather not think about. One wishes for an only grandchild to run and play, to graduate from college, to marry and succeed, not to … (see, I can't even say it!!!!!!)

The shock and horror that followed Don's death are something I would rather not recount: Calling our children to report the news, watching the baby's body, small as a loaf of bread, as it was zipped into a heavy plastic bag — these images have nothing to do with the merriment of Christmas, and I hope my mention of them will not dampen your spirits at this, the most special and glittering time of the year.

The evening of December sixteenth was a very dark hour for the Dunbar family. At least with Khe Sahn in police custody we could grieve privately, consoling ourselves with the belief that justice had been carried out.

How foolish we were!!!!!!!!!

The bitter tears were still wet upon our faces when the police returned to Tiffany Circle, where they began their ruthless questioning of Yours Truly!!!!!!!!!!!! Through the aid of an interpreter, Khe Sahn had spent a sleepless night at police headquarters, constructing a story of unspeakable lies and betrayal!

While I am not at liberty to discuss her exact testimony, allow me to voice my disappointment that anyone (let alone the police!) would even *think* of taking Khe Sahn's word over my own. How could I have placed a helpless child in the washing machine? Even if I were cruel enough to do such a thing, when would I have found the time? I was out shopping.

You may have read that our so-called "neighbor" Cherise Clarmont-Shea reported that she witnessed me leaving my home at around one-fifteen on the afternoon of December sixteenth and then, twenty minutes later, allegedly park my car on the far corner of Tiffany and Papageorge and, in her words, "creep" through her backyard and in through my basement door!!!!!! Cherise Clarmont-Shea certainly understands the meaning of the word *creep*, doesn't she? She's been married to one for so long that she has turned into something of a creep herself!! If the makeup she applies is any indication of her vision, then I believe it is safe to say she can't see two inches in front of her, much less testify to the identity of someone she might think she's seen crossing her yard. She's on pills, everyone knows that. She's desperate for attention and I might pity her under different circumstances. I did not return home early and creep through the Shea's unkept backyard, but even if I had, what possible motive would I have had? Why would I, as certain people have been suggesting, want to murder my own grandchild? This is madness, pure and simple. And the others who have made statements against me, Chaz Staple and Vivian Taps, they were both at home during a weekday afternoon doing guess what while their spouses were hard at work. What are *they* hiding?

These charges are ridiculous, yet I must take them seriously as my very life may be at stake! Listening to a taped translation of Khe Sahn's police statement, the Dunbar family has come to fully understand the meaning of the words "controlling," "vindictive," "manipulative," "greedy," and, in a spiritual sense, "ugly."

Not exactly the words one wishes to toss about during the Christmas season!!!!!!!!

A hearing has been set for December twenty-seventh and, knowing how disappointed you, our friends, might feel at being left out, I have included the time and address at the bottom of this letter. The hearing is an opportunity during which you might convey your belated Christmas spirit through deed and action. Given the opportunity to defend *your* character I would not hesitate and I know you must feel the exact same way toward me. That heartfelt concern, that desire to stand by your friends and family, is the very foundation upon which we celebrate the Christmas season, isn't it?

While this year's Dunbar Christmas will be seasoned with loss and sadness, we plan to proceed, as best we can, toward that day of days, December twenty-seventh — 1:45 P.M. at The White Paw County Courthouse, room 412.

I will be calling to remind you of that information and look forward to discussing the festive bounty of your holiday season.

Until that time we wish the best to you and yours.

Merry Christmas,

The Dunbars

NEW PLAYS

★ **CLOSER by Patrick Marber.** Winner of the 1998 Olivier Award for Best Play and the 1999 New York Drama Critics Circle Award for Best Foreign Play. Four lives intertwine over the course of four and a half years in this densely plotted, stinging look at modern love and betrayal. "CLOSER is a sad, savvy, often funny play that casts a steely, unblinking gaze at the world of relationships and lets you come to your own conclusions ... CLOSER does not merely hold your attention; it burrows into you." *–New York Magazine* "A powerful, darkly funny play about the cosmic collision between the sun of love and the comet of desire." *–Newsweek Magazine* [2M, 2W] ISBN: 0-8222-1722-8

★ **THE MOST FABULOUS STORY EVER TOLD by Paul Rudnick.** A stage manager, headset and prompt book at hand, brings the house lights to half, then dark, and cues the creation of the world. Throughout the play, she's in control of everything. In other words, she's either God, or she thinks she is. "Line by line, Mr. Rudnick may be the funniest writer for the stage in the United States today ... One-liners, epigrams, withering put-downs and flashing repartee: These are the candles that Mr. Rudnick lights instead of cursing the darkness ... a testament to the virtues of laughing ... and in laughter, there is something like the memory of Eden." *–The NY Times* "Funny it is ... consistently, rapaciously, deliriously ... easily the funniest play in town." *–Variety* [4M, 5W] ISBN: 0-8222-1720-1

★ **A DOLL'S HOUSE by Henrik Ibsen, adapted by Frank McGuinness.** Winner of the 1997 Tony Award for Best Revival. "New, raw, gut-twisting and gripping. Easily the hottest drama this season." *–USA Today* "Bold, brilliant and alive." *–The Wall Street Journal* "A thunderclap of an evening that takes your breath away." *–Time Magazine* [4M, 4W, 2 boys] ISBN: 0-8222-1636-1

★ **THE HERBAL BED by Peter Whelan.** The play is based on actual events which occurred in Stratford-upon-Avon in the summer of 1613, when William Shakespeare's elder daughter was publicly accused of having a sexual liaison with a married neighbor and family friend. "In his probing new play, THE HERBAL BED ... Peter Whelan muses about a sidelong event in the life of Shakespeare's family and creates a finely textured tapestry of love and lies in the early 17th-century Stratford." *–The NY Times* "It is a first rate drama with interesting moral issues of truth and expediency." *–The NY Post* [5M, 3W] ISBN: 0-8222-1675-2

★ **SNAKEBIT by David Marshall Grant.** A study of modern friendship when put to the test. "... a rather smart and absorbing evening of water-cooler theater, the intimate sort of Off-Broadway experience that has you picking apart the recognizable characters long after the curtain calls." *– The NY Times* "Off-Broadway keeps on presenting us with compelling reasons for going to the theater. The latest is SNAKEBIT, David Marshall Grant's smart new comic drama about being thirtysomething and losing one's way in life." *–The NY Daily News* [3M, 1W] ISBN: 0-8222-1724-4

★ **A QUESTION OF MERCY by David Rabe.** The Obie Award-winning playwright probes the sensitive and controversial issue of doctor-assisted suicide in the age of AIDS in this poignant drama. "There are many devastating ironies in Mr. Rabe's beautifully considered, piercingly clear-eyed work ..." *–The NY Times* "With unsettling candor and disturbing insight, the play arouses pity and understanding of a troubling subject ... Rabe's provocative tale is an affirmation of dignity that rings clear and true." *–Variety* [6M, 1W] ISBN: 0-8222-1643-4

★ **DIMLY PERCEIVED THREATS TO THE SYSTEM by Jon Klein.** Reality and fantasy overlap with hilarious results as this unforgettable family attempts to survive the nineties. "Here's a play whose point about fractured families goes to the heart, mind – and ears." *–The Washington Post* "... an end-of-the millennium comedy about a family on the verge of a nervous breakdown ... Trenchant and hilarious ..." *–The Baltimore Sun* [2M, 4W] ISBN: 0-8222-1677-9

DRAMATISTS PLAY SERVICE, INC.
440 Park Avenue South, New York, NY 10016 212-683-8960 Fax 212-213-1539
postmaster@dramatists.com www.dramatists.com

NEW PLAYS

★ **AS BEES IN HONEY DROWN by Douglas Carter Beane.** Winner of the John Gassner Playwriting Award. A hot young novelist finds the subject of his new screenplay in a New York socialite who leads him into the world of *Auntie Mame* and *Breakfast at Tiffany's*, before she takes him for a ride. "A delicious soufflé of a satire … [an] extremely entertaining fable for an age that always chooses image over substance." *–The NY Times* "… A witty assessment of one of the most active and relentless industries in a consumer society … the creation of 'hot' young things, which the media have learned to mass produce with efficiency and zeal." *–The NY Daily News* [3M, 3W, flexible casting] ISBN: 0-8222-1651-5

★ **STUPID KIDS by John C. Russell.** In rapid, highly stylized scenes, the story follows four high-school students as they make their way from first through eighth period and beyond, struggling with the fears, frustrations, and longings peculiar to youth. "In STUPID KIDS … playwright John C. Russell gets the opera of adolescence to a T … The stylized teenspeak of STUPID KIDS … suggests that Mr. Russell may have hidden a tape recorder under a desk in study hall somewhere and then scoured the tapes for good quotations … it is the kids' insular, ceaselessly churning world, a pre-adult world of Doritos and libidos, that the playwright seeks to lay bare." *–The NY Times* "STUPID KIDS [is] a sharp-edged … whoosh of teen angst and conformity anguish. It is also very funny." *–NY Newsday* [2M, 2W] ISBN: 0-8222-1698-1

★ **COLLECTED STORIES by Donald Margulies.** From Obie Award-winner Donald Margulies comes a provocative analysis of a student-teacher relationship that turns sour when the protégé becomes a rival. "With his fine ear for detail, Margulies creates an authentic, insular world, and he gives equal weight to the opposing viewpoints of two formidable characters." *–The LA Times* "This is probably Margulies' best play to date …" *–The NY Post* "… always fluid and lively, the play is thick with ideas, like a stock-pot of good stew." *–The Village Voice* [2W] ISBN: 0-8222-1640-X

★ **FREEDOMLAND by Amy Freed.** An overdue showdown between a son and his father sets off fireworks that illuminate the neurosis, rage and anxiety of one family – and of America at the turn of the millennium. "FREEDOMLAND's more obvious links are to *Buried Child* and *Bosoms and Neglect*. Freed, like Guare, is an inspired wordsmith with a gift for surreal touches in situations grounded in familiar and real territory." *–Curtain Up* [3M, 4W] ISBN: 0-8222-1719-8

★ **STOP KISS by Diana Son.** A poignant and funny play about the ways, both sudden and slow, that lives can change irrevocably. "There's so much that is vital and exciting about STOP KISS … you want to embrace this young author and cheer her onto other works … the writing on display here is funny and credible … you also will be charmed by its heartfelt characters and up-to-the-minute humor." *–The NY Daily News* "… irresistibly exciting … a sweet, sad, and enchantingly sincere play." *–The NY Times* [3M, 3W] ISBN: 0-8222-1731-7

★ **THREE DAYS OF RAIN by Richard Greenberg.** The sins of fathers and mothers make for a bittersweet elegy in this poignant and revealing drama. "… a work so perfectly judged it heralds the arrival of a major playwright … Greenberg is extraordinary." *–The NY Daily News* "Greenberg's play is filled with graceful passages that are by turns melancholy, harrowing, and often, quite funny." *–Variety* [2M, 1W] ISBN: 0-8222-1676-0

★ **THE WEIR by Conor McPherson.** In a bar in rural Ireland, the local men swap spooky stories in an attempt to impress a young woman from Dublin who recently moved into a nearby "haunted" house. However, the tables are soon turned when she spins a yarn of her own. "You shed all sense of time at this beautiful and devious new play." *–The NY Times* "Sheer theatrical magic. I have rarely been so convinced that I have just seen a modern classic. Tremendous." *–The London Daily Telegraph* [4M, 1W] ISBN: 0-8222-1706-6

DRAMATISTS PLAY SERVICE, INC.
440 Park Avenue South, New York, NY 10016 212-683-8960 Fax 212-213-1539
postmaster@dramatists.com   www.dramatists.com